Little Mitchie

TERMITES THAT BUILD TOWERS

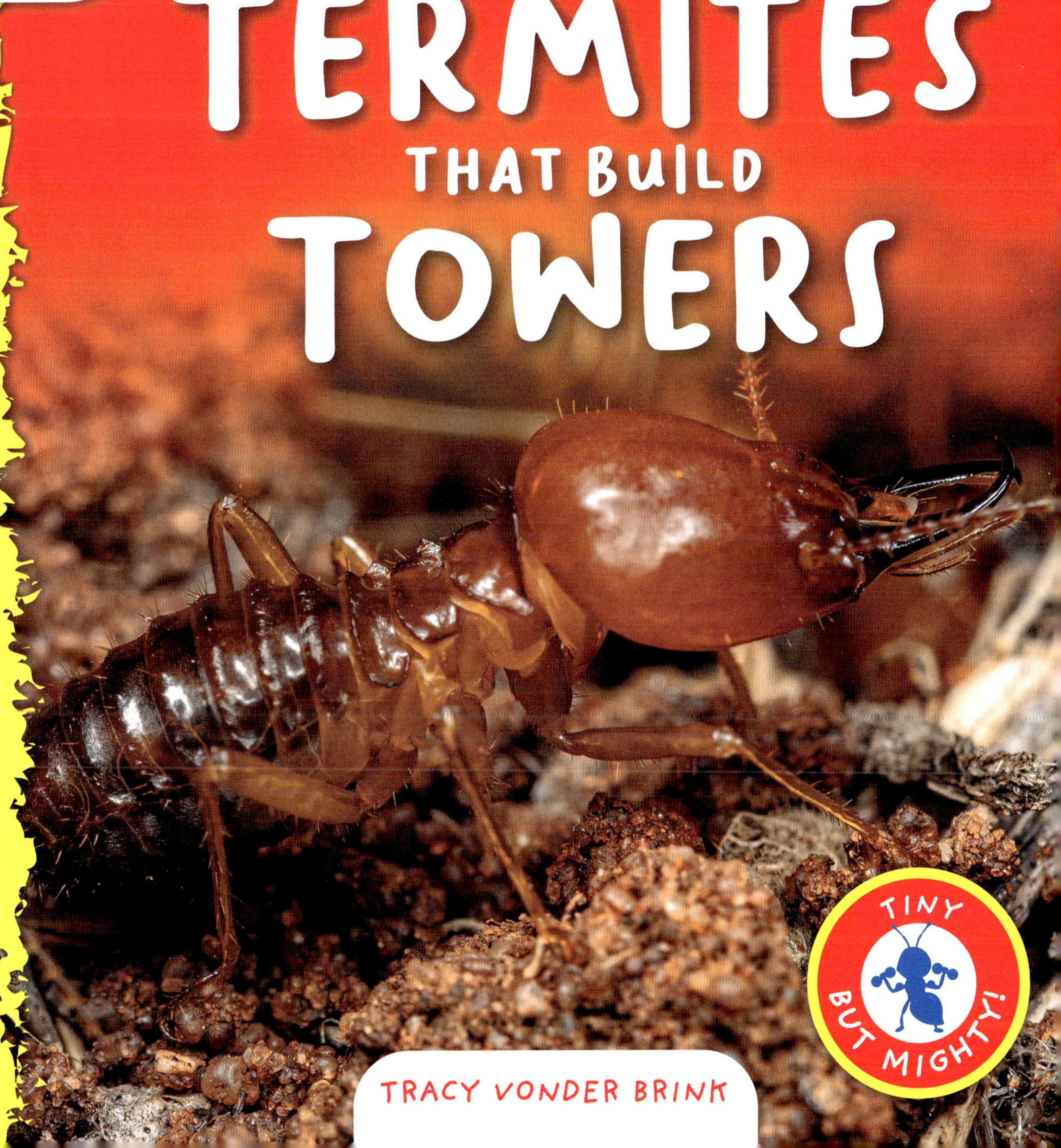

TINY BUT MIGHTY!

TRACY VONDER BRINK

CREATING YOUNG NONFICTION READERS

Little Mitchie books spark curiosity and support early nonfiction reading for students in Grades 2-3. Designed to build vocabulary, support second language learners, and prepare readers for middle-grade content, each book includes helpful tips for parents and educators to build confidence and deepen understanding of the world.

TIPS FOR READING NONFICTION WITH BEGINNING READERS

Talk about Nonfiction

Begin by explaining that nonfiction books give us information that is true. The book will be organized around a specific topic or idea, and we may learn new facts through reading.

Look at the Parts

Most nonfiction books have helpful features. Our *Little Mitchie* titles include color photographs and graphic aids, a table of contents, a glossary, and an index. Share the purpose of these features with your reader.

Color Photos and Graphic Aids

A lot of information can be found by "reading" photos, charts, maps, and other graphic aids found within nonfiction texts. Help your reader learn more about the different ways information can be displayed.

Table of Contents

Located at the front of the book, this list shows the big ideas within the text and the page numbers where they can be found.

Glossary

Located at the back of the book, the glossary defines key words and phrases that are related to the topic. These words and phrases can be found in the text in colored type.

Index

Located at the back of the book, an index is an alphabetical list of topics and the page numbers where they can be found.

With a little help and guidance about reading nonfiction, you can feel good about introducing a young reader to the world of *Little Mitchie* nonfiction books.

Little Mitchie is an imprint of:

Mitchell Lane
PUBLISHERS

2001 SW 31st Avenue
Hallandale, FL 33009
mitchelllanepub.com

First Edition, 2027.

Author: Tracy Vonder Brink
Designer: Jen Bowers
Editor: Tricia Hoffman

Library of Congress Cataloging-in-Publication Data
Title: Termites That Build Towers / by Tracy Vonder Brink

Description: Hallandale, FL :
Mitchell Lane Publishers, [2027]

Identifiers:
ISBN 979-8-89260-889-3 (library bound)
ISBN 979-8-89260-992-0 (eBook)

Library of Congress Control Number: 2026936382

PHOTO CREDITS
Shutterstock: cover, p.1 ©2022 Vinicius R. Souza, p.5 ©2012 Janelle Lugge, p.6 ©2017 Hennadii Filchakov, p.9, 22 ©2017 chakkrachai nicharat, p.10–11 ©2016 7th Son Studio, p.13, 22 ©2008 Susan Flashman, p.14 ©2016 chakkrachai nicharat, p.16–17 ©2019 Designua, ©2016 PK289, p.19, 22 ©2022 AgriTech, p.20 ©2015 Peter van Dam

TABLE OF CONTENTS

Chapter One

MIGHTY MOUND BUILDERS

Termite **mounds** can stand nine feet (3 m) to almost 30 feet (9 m) tall! The mound isn't their home, though. Termites live in a large nest underneath.

MIGHTY MOMENT

Not all termites build mounds. The kinds that do live in grasslands from Africa to Australia.

Mound-building termites are approximately as big as a grain of rice. How do these tiny creatures build such tall towers? Why do they build them if they don't live there?

Chapter Two

MAKING MOUNDS

Termites use their **mandibles** to build mounds. They gather bits of soil and wood and glue them together with their **saliva** and poop. Then they pile them up into mounds.

MIGHTY MOMENT

Termites have different jobs. Workers build and fix the mound and nest. Some find food. Others care for the eggs and young. Soldiers protect the mound and nest. The king mates with the queen, and she lays eggs.

Mounds are built around a **hollow** tunnel in the middle. It looks like a **chimney**. It goes from the termites' nest to the top of the mound. Smaller tunnels inside the mound connect to the chimney. Tunnels also go into the nest.

MIGHTY MOMENT

Termite nests have many tunnels and **chambers**. Termites raise their young in the chambers and also store food there. They grow fungus in some chambers, like a garden.

Chapter Three

AIR IN, AIR OUT

Termites breathe air just like you do. How do they have air when their nests are underneath the mound?

MIGHTY MOMENT
The oldest known termite mound is in South Africa. Termites have lived in it for 34,000 years!

Air comes into the mound through tiny holes in its walls. The mound warms and cools during the day and night. This temperature change causes air inside the chimney and nest to rise and fall. This **circulates** air through the nest.

The movement brings fresh air into the nest and carries old air out. That means the mound works a bit like your lungs do when you breathe in and out!

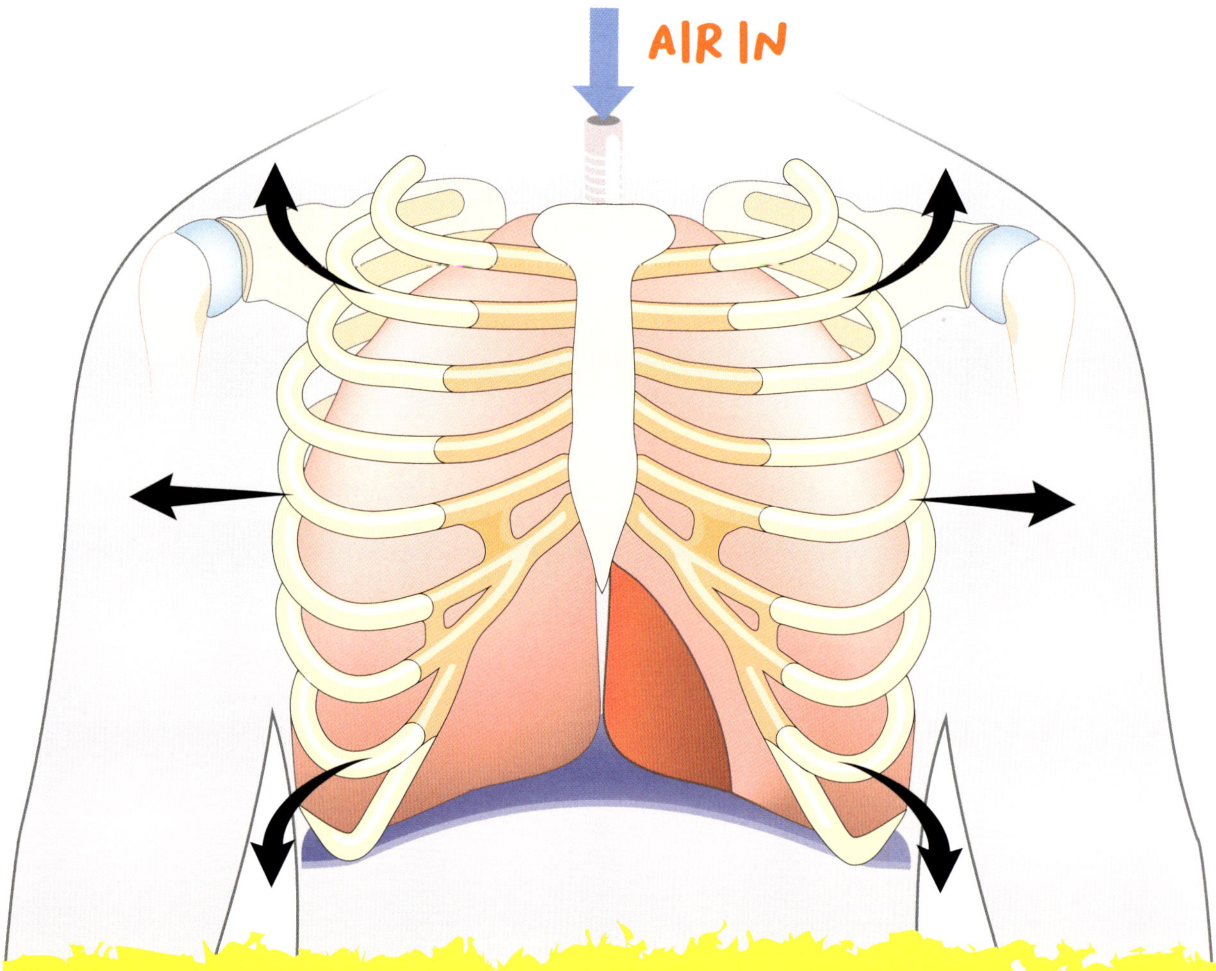

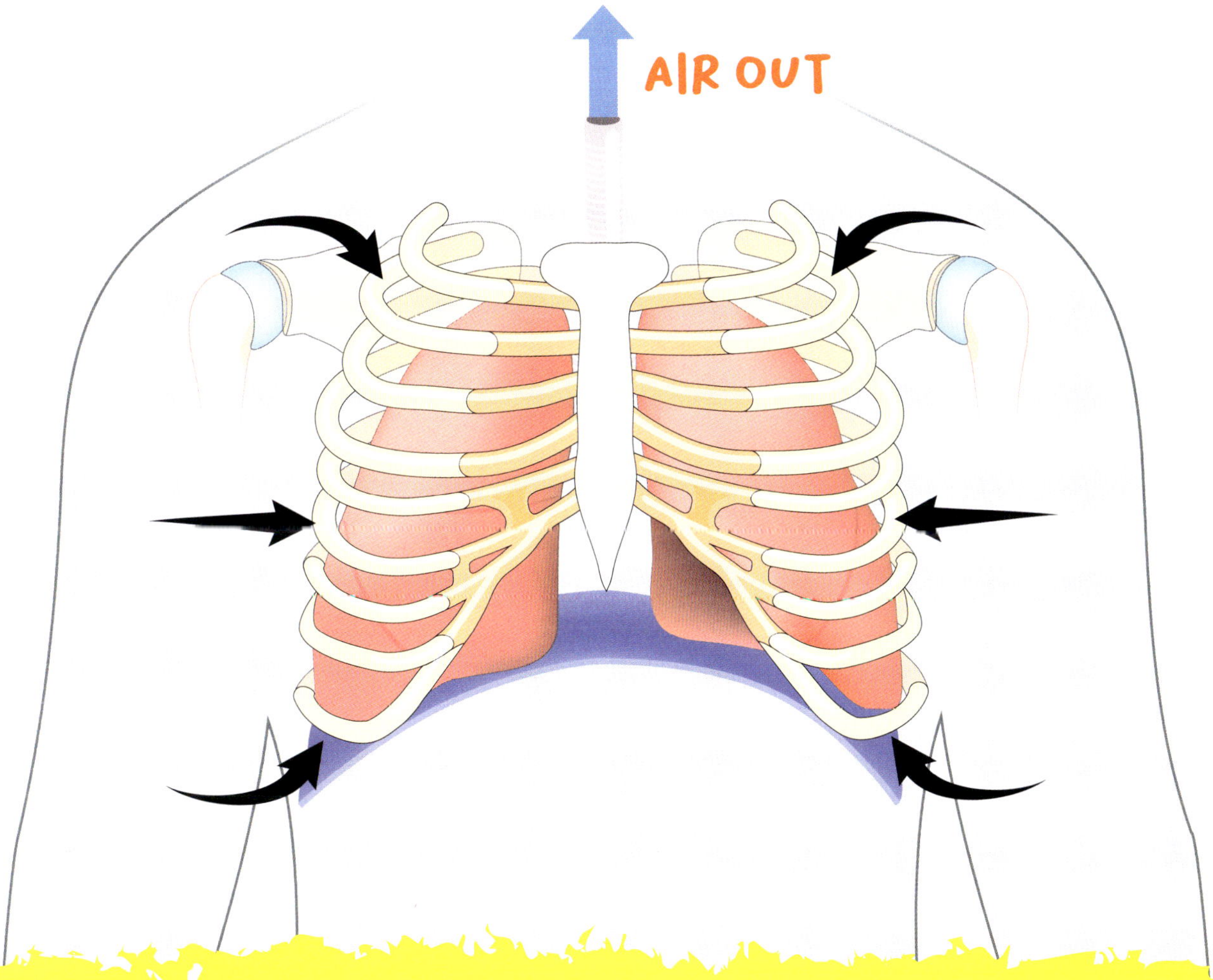
AIR OUT

Chapter Four

TERRIFIC TERMITES

Termites may not live in the mound, but it helps them live by bringing fresh air into the nest. The mound also protects the nest by keeping out rain and predators.

MIGHTY MOMENT

Not all termites eat wood. Some kinds eat grasses. Some mound-building termites eat the fungus they grow in their nests.

Termite mounds also help other animals. Some birds build nests inside the mounds. Mongoose families live there too. Tiny termites make a big difference!

A CLOSER LOOK

Worker termites' mandibles are made to chew, dig, and carry. Soldiers' mandibles are made to fight.

Termites that grow fungus are like farmers. They care for the fungus and help it grow.

A group of more than 200 million termite mounds was found in Brazil. It covers an area the size of Great Britain!

GLOSSARY

chambers (chaym-burz) rooms

chimney (chim-nee) a tall pipe on a house that carries smoke from a fireplace up to the sky

circulates (sur-kyuh-lates) moves around in a circle

hollow (hah-loh) empty on the inside

mandibles (man-duh-buhls) the biting mouthparts of some insects

mound (mound) a hill or pile of something

saliva (suh-lye-vuh) spit, or the clear liquid made by the mouth

FURTHER READING

Becker, Trudy. *Termites.* North Star Editions, 2025.

Brody, Walt. *How Is a Building Like a Termite Mound?* Lerner Publications, 2022.

ON THE INTERNET

Termite
https://kids.nationalgeographic.com/animals/invertebrates/facts/termite
National Geographic Kids shares where and how termites live.

Termite
https://kids.britannica.com/kids/article/termite/353849
Learn how big termites are, how many eggs a termite queen lays, and much more with Britannica Kids.

INDEX